The Greatest Bible Stories Ever Told
Special Families

Stephen Elkins
AUTHOR

Tim O'Connor
ILLUSTRATIONS

BROADMAN
&HOLMAN
PUBLISHERS
NASHVILLE, TENNESSEE

ADAM AND EVE

Genesis 1:27 (And) God created man in his image,...
male and female he created them.

The Lord God used the dust of the
ground to create Adam, the first man.
When God breathed His breath of life
into Adam's nose, he became
a living soul.

The Lord placed Adam in a beautiful
garden called Eden. It was a perfect
home. Adam was given the
special job of taking
care of all God
had made.

Then the Lord said to Adam, "You may eat the fruit from any tree in the garden except one. Do not eat from that tree." And God warned Adam that if he disobeyed and ate the fruit, he would die.

So Adam did the things God asked him to do.

Then the Lord said, "It is not good for Adam to be alone. I will make him a helper and friend." So the Lord caused Adam to fall asleep. God then removed one of Adam's ribs and from it He made a woman.

God brought the woman to Adam and he was very pleased. Together Adam and Eve took care of the garden and worshiped God.

The Lord created every beast of the field and every bird in the sky and brought them to Adam one by one. Adam gave each one of them a name.

He gave names to all the cattle, to the birds of the air, and to every beast of the field.

Affirmation: What a wonderful God we serve!

ABRAHAM AND SARAH'S SURPRISE
Genesis 18:14 Is anything too hard for the Lord (to do)?

Noah's oldest son, Shem, had hundreds of descendants born many years later. One was named Abram. Abram was a righteous man who married a beautiful woman named Sarai. One day the Lord spoke to Abram and said, "Leave your country, your family, and neighbors and go to a land I will show you. There I will bless you and make you into a great nation."

So Abram obeyed the Lord and set out on a journey with his wife Sarai and his nephew, Lot. One night the Lord appeared to Abram and said, "Look up at the night sky and count the stars. One day your family shall number more than that!" Abram was very puzzled by what the Lord had said for he and Sarai were growing old and had no children.

When Abram was 99 years old, the Lord appeared to him again and said, "Abram, I make this promise to you. You will be called the father of many nations, and you shall be called Abraham and your wife shall be called Sarah.

For I will bless her with a son and you will call his name Isaac. And I will give to you and your children this land. I will care for you and be your God." Abraham laughed and said, "How can a son be born to people our age?"

Sarah overheard what the Lord had said to her husband and she, too, laughed and laughed! "How can this be?" she giggled.

But the Lord heard her laughter and said, "Is anything too hard for the Lord? I will return next year and you, Sarah, will have a son."

When Abraham was 100 years old, Sarah had a little baby boy named Isaac, just as God had promised.

Affirmation: There is nothing too hard for the Lord to do!

A RAISIN CAKE

Song of Solomon 2:5 Sustain me with raisin cakes.

King Solomon wrote many songs and poems for the wife he loved. He knew that his marriage vows were very serious and that lasting love requires a little work. So he worked at it. He knew that romantic love can draw two people together, but only the Lord can make it last forever. Therefore, Solomon wrote this simple poem to his wife.

How beautiful you are, my darling.
Oh, how beautiful are your eyes.
You are like a lily among thorns
*   compared to other girls.*
Strengthen me with raisin cakes,
Refresh me with apples,
For I have grown tired
*   and I love sitting with you.*
Oh, how beautiful you are, my darling.
Oh, how beautiful are your eyes.

Affirmation:
The Lord will
sustain me!

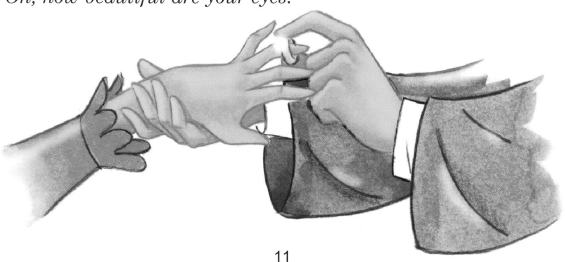

The BIRTH of JESUS

GABRIEL'S VISIT

Luke 1:13a But the angel said to him, "Do not be afraid, Zachariah; your prayer has been heard."

Now this is how the birth of Jesus Christ came about. In the days when Herod was king of Judea, there lived a priest named Zacharias. He had a wonderful wife named Elizabeth. They had grown old together but had no children.

One day Zacharias was in the temple preparing an offering to the Lord when suddenly, an angel appeared before him.

Zacharias was afraid! "Do not be afraid, for God has heard your prayers. Soon you and Elizabeth will have a baby boy. You are to name him John, for he will be a great man of God. Because of his preaching many will repent and turn back to God. He will prepare the way for the coming of the Lord."

Zacharias said to the angel, "How can this be true? I am too old to have children and so is my wife."

"I am Gabriel, a messenger sent by God to tell you this wonderful news. But since you have not believed me, you shall be unable to speak until all of these things have happened." Then as quickly as he had come, Gabriel disappeared.

Outside the temple, the people were waiting for Zacharias, wondering what was keeping him. Finally, he came out, unable to speak. He used sign language to try to tell them what had happened. They thought he had seen a vision!

Finally, a silent Zacharias returned home. Soon Elizabeth discovered that she was going to have a baby, just as Gabriel had said.

Now sometime later, Gabriel was sent by God to the city of Nazareth to visit a young woman named Mary. She was engaged to marry a carpenter named Joseph.

But before their wedding day, Gabriel came to her and said, "Hello favored one, the Lord is with you!" Mary had never heard such a greeting before and wondered, "What does it mean?"

Gabriel spoke again, "Do not be afraid Mary, for I have a message for you from the Lord. You are going to have a baby boy and you shall call His name Jesus. He will be great and will be called the Son of God, and His kingdom will have no end!"

Mary was confused. "How can this be?" she asked. "I have no husband yet."

Gabriel answered, "Nothing is impossible with God. Even Elizabeth your relative is going to have a baby, though she is very old. For nothing will be impossible with God."

"I am the servant of the Lord," said Mary. "Let all that you have said be done in my life." And in an instant, the angel was gone.

Mary couldn't wait to tell Elizabeth about Gabriel's visit. She left Nazareth at once and hurried through the hills of Judah. When she arrived at Zacharias' house, she hurried inside and called, "Elizabeth! It's me, Mary." When Elizabeth heard Mary's voice, her baby jumped inside her and the Spirit of God filled her. "How blessed you are, Mary, to be the mother of my Lord."

Mary wondered, "How could Elizabeth know about the baby Jesus? I haven't told her yet." Mary said, "I am happy because God is my Lord and Savior. Holy is His name." Mary stayed with Elizabeth for three months and then she returned home.

JOHN IS BORN

Luke 1:63   He asked for a writing tablet, and to everyone's astonishment he wrote, "His name is John."

Time passed and soon Elizabeth's baby was born. Their friends and church leaders wanted to name the child Zacharias, like his father. But Elizabeth said, "No, his name will be John."

"You can't call him John," they said. "Let's ask Zacharias what the child's name will be." On a tablet Zacharias wrote, "His name is John." At that very moment, Zacharias could once again speak. And oh, how he praised the Lord! "This must be a very special child," the people said, "for the hand of the Lord is upon him."

Affirmation: I will praise the Lord!

20

JESUS IS BORN

Matthew 1:21 And you shall call His name Jesus, for He will save His people from their sins.

When Mary told Joseph all of the things that had happened to her and Elizabeth, he was very confused. But one night as he slept, an angel of the Lord appeared to him in a dream and said, "Mary is a good woman. Do not put her away. Take her as your wife, for her baby is a miracle baby that God Himself has given her."

"And you shall call His name Jesus, for He will save His people from their sins."

When Joseph awoke from his dream, he did exactly what the angel asked him to do. He took Mary as his wife and he never doubted again.

Now it came about that the Roman king, Caesar Augustus, wanted to know how many people were living in his kingdom. So everyone, including Joseph and Mary, had to return to their own city to be counted. Mary was ready to have her baby, but still they made the journey from Nazareth to the city of David which is called Bethlehem.

When they arrived in Bethlehem, it was very crowded. Mary was ready to give birth, and though Joseph looked everywhere for a room, there was none to be found. Finally, Joseph and Mary came to a stable where sheep and livestock were kept. There, Jesus Christ, the Son of God, was born. And Mary wrapped Him in swaddling clothes and laid Him in a manger, which is a feeding box. There, under the stars of Bethlehem, the baby Jesus slept.

Nearby, there was a group of shepherds keeping watch over their flocks of sheep.

Suddenly, an angel of the Lord appeared before them and the darkness was filled with light! The shepherds were so afraid!

Then the angel spoke. "Do not be afraid, for I bring you good news of a great joy! Today in Bethlehem, your Savior is born who is Christ the Lord."

"Come and see the Lord! You will know it is He when you find the baby wrapped in swaddling clothes and lying in a manger."

Then suddenly, many angels appeared before them, praising God and saying, "Glory to God in the highest. And on earth, peace among men with whom He is pleased."

When the angels departed, the shepherds said, "Let's go to Bethlehem right now to see this thing that has happened." So they hurried into town and found their way to Mary and Joseph. And just as the angel had said, they found Christ the Lord lying in a manger.

Now when they had seen all this, they told everyone about Jesus and the appearance of angels. The shepherds went back to their flocks, praising God all the way!

Affirmation: I love Jesus!

THE BAPTISM OF JESUS

Matthew 3:13   Then Jesus came from Galilee to the Jordan to be baptized by John.

Zacharias and Elizabeth's baby boy grew to be a very rugged man. He became known as John the Baptist and he lived and preached in the desert.
For food he ate locusts and wild honey, and he wore a coat of camel hair.

His message was very simple, "Repent! Stop doing evil things and return to God's ways, for the kingdom of heaven is coming soon."

Many people would come to John and be baptized in the Jordan River. They would tell God how sorry they were for not obeying Him and promised to live for Him.

Then one day as John stood in the Jordan River, he saw Jesus walking towards him to be baptized. John knew that Jesus had never sinned and did not need to be baptized. So John said, "It is I who needs to be baptized by You. Why do You come to me?"

Jesus replied, "It is important that you baptize Me now. By doing this, we show others the right thing to do."

When Jesus came up out of the water, the heavens opened, and the Spirit of God came down upon Him like a dove. Then a voice came from heaven saying, "This is My Son. I love Him and I am very pleased with Him."

Affirmation: I will love and obey Jesus!

I'VE GOT HOSPITALITY

3 John 1:8 We ought to show hospitality to (Christians) so that we may work together for truth.

In John's third letter he writes to his dear Christian friend named Gaius. He says many kind things to Gaius to encourage him. Gaius was living his life in a way that pleased Jesus. Perhaps his greatest gift was that of hospitality. He would always take care of the missionaries who came to visit his church. He made sure they had a warm meal and a place to sleep. We, too, ought to show hospitality to our Christian friends and workers.

Affirmation: I will show my hospitality by saying a kind word to a Christian worker this week!

COLLECT ALL 10

Word & Song AUDIO BOOK

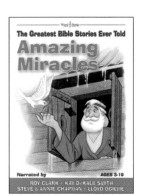
The Greatest Bible Stories Ever Told
Amazing Miracles
Narrated by AGES 3-10
ROY CLARK · KAY DeKALB SMITH
STEVE & ANNIE CHAPMAN · LLOYD OGILVIE
0-8054-2471-7

The Greatest Bible Stories Ever Told
God's Power
Narrated by AGES 3-10
LLOYD OGILVIE · DEAN STONE
GEORGE BEVERLY SHEA
0-8054-2466-0

The Greatest Bible Stories Ever Told
Stories of Faith
AGES 3-10
LARNELLE HARRIS
STEVE & ANNIE CHAPMAN · LLOYD OGILVIE
0-8054-2470-9

The Greatest Bible Stories Ever Told
Build Character
Narrated by AGES 3-10
LARNELLE HARRIS · STEVE GREEN
LLOYD OGILVIE
0-8054-2469-5

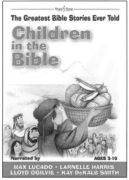
The Greatest Bible Stories Ever Told
Children in the Bible
Narrated by AGES 3-10
MAX LUCADO · LARNELLE HARRIS
LLOYD OGILVIE · KAY DeKALB SMITH
0-8054-2474-1

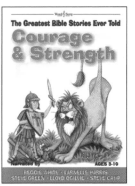
The Greatest Bible Stories Ever Told
Courage & Strength
Narrated by AGES 3-10
REGGIE WHITE · LARNELLE HARRIS
STEVE GREEN · LLOYD OGILVIE · STEVE CAMP
0-8054-2468-7

The Greatest Bible Stories Ever Told
Friendship & Kindness
Narrated by AGES 3-10
MAX LUCADO · REBECCA ST JAMES
LARNELLE HARRIS · TWILA PARIS · STEVE GREEN
0-8054-2473-3

The Greatest Bible Stories Ever Told
The Good Shepherd
Narrated by AGES 3-10
STEVE GREEN
JERRY FALWELL · ANNIE CHAPMAN
0-8054-2475-X

The Greatest Bible Stories Ever Told
Prayer & Promise
Narrated by AGES 3-10
MAX LUCADO · GEORGE BEVERLY SHEA
STEVE GREEN · ADRIAN ROGERS · LLOYD OGILVIE
0-8054-2472-5

Available in Your Favorite Christian Bookstore.

The Greatest Bible Stories Ever Told
Special Families
JONI EARECKSON TADA · TWILA PARIS · STEVE GREEN
LLOYD OGILVIE · STEVE & ANNIE CHAPMAN
0-8054-2467-9

We hope you enjoyed this Word & Song Storybook.